Policing in Massillon, Ohio;
"Protect & Swerve"

Author: Sgt Brian Muntean (Retired)

This book is dedicated to my Grandmother (Dolores Marchand) who was an amazing writer. She was certainly a positive influence in my life, and we all miss her dearly. In addition, I wrote this book simply because I wanted to tell the story about my journey as a law enforcement officer in Massillon, Ohio. Although my twenty-five years of service have passed, I wanted to perhaps influence future law enforcement officers who may be traveling similar paths that I took in life. We owe them everything as they protect all of us during their careers.

Photo: My grandmother (Dolores Marchand)

Table of Contents

Chapter One: "Mom, I Wanna Be a Cop"

Chapter Two: "Life Before Police Work"

Chapter Three: "Life as a Rookie"

Chapter Four: "Midnights"

Chapter Five: "Off-Duty"

Chapter Six: "Leadership"

Chapter Seven: "Stories from the Streets"

Chapter Eight: "Signal Two"

Chapter One
"Mom, I Wanna be a Cop"

Well, where do I start? Like most cops, I decided long ago at the age of thirteen that I was going to become a police officer. I was fixated on becoming one. Nobody was going to tell me I could not do it. Growing up in Canton, OH, I would often see the ol' "black & whites" driving around town. I would see uniformed officers from Canton P.D. working the parade route all hours of the night in "Hall of Fame City". I would see the deputy sheriffs patrolling the back roads of Stark County. I would see the Troopers from the Ohio State Highway Patrol sitting in the median along I-77 looking for speeders.

Photo: Route 800 cuts right through Canton South

When I saw a uniformed law enforcement officer, I was in awe. As a young, naïve boy, I really did look at them as "super heroes". I thought to myself, "That's what I want to be when I grow up". It seemed like a career and not just a job. I saw excitement. I saw pride. I loved the idea of wearing a uniform. I loved the thought of being able to "right a wrong". I loved thinking I would have the ability to stand up for those who could not stand up for themselves. I loved being able to make someone pay for their wrongdoings. Little did I know that although I would see all of this during my law enforcement career, I would also see things that I never planned on seeing.

I remember telling my mother that I wanted to be a police officer. I have to say she was not thrilled. She wanted me to become a math teacher. I truly understood her motherly concerns. Nobody wants to bury their son. But I was fixated. Again, nobody was going to tell me any different. That's what I was going to do. Although my mother always gave me good advice, I like to believe that she is proud of the fact that two of her four sons became law enforcement officers. After twenty-five years as a police officer, I have to say that entering this profession was one of the best decisions I ever made, bar none. It was much more than a job. It's was an education. Believe me when I say that you cannot learn this stuff in a classroom.

I'll be honest with you and tell you that there probably isn't a more difficult job to get than that of a police officer. There are many steps during the hiring process. In a nutshell, if you don't really want to be a police officer, then choose another employment path. I tell people that because it's not a job that you can do for twenty-five years unless you really have a passion for it. The application process alone is tedious enough to cause a potential applicant to shy away if they really aren't serious about it. As a general rule, you have to take a civil service exam, a physical agility test, a psychological exam, a polygraph, and then be subjected to a background investigation where an investigator will look deep into your background to try to determine if you're suited for a law enforcement career. Case in point: I worked as a "bagboy" at Fisher's Foods when I was a senior at Canton South High School. I always tell people that I was the worst bagboy in Stark County. I had a very short attention span, and I was at the age where all I did was look at girls. Well, my buddy and I put a note in an "older woman's" grocery bag offering her our phone number. That one went really bad. Her husband showed up a few hours later. He wasn't too happy. Yep. You guessed it. That incident ended up in my background investigation years later. They basically find out everything that you ever did.

We've all done bad things in our lives. They're not looking for angels. Just try to minimize the bad decisions. Oh, and don't hit on married women.

Many would ask themselves how they prepare themselves for a law enforcement career. There are many things one can do to increase their chances of getting hired. Should one go to college? Should they join the military? Should they go to the academy? Well, first and foremost, I would say that one should make good decisions while growing up. Again, nobody expects to hire an angel, but a pattern of bad behavior would be a "red flag" to any agency whether that pattern of behavior is a bad driving record, a criminal record, bad credit, or a poor employment record. Also, stay away from "shady" friends. It's been my experience that when good people hang out with bad people or hang out in bad places, bad things tend to happen to them. Increase your chance of good things happening to you by associating yourself with good people and hanging out at reputable places. It's a pretty simple formula for success.

Military service is probably the one single thing that will prepare you for police work more than anything else. There are many reasons for that. It prepares you in so many different ways. You develop discipline. You learn about teamwork. You learn about goals. You learn about pride.

I joined the Army National Guard at the age of nineteen because I needed a way to pay my tuition at Kent State University. Joining the military was probably the single best decision that I ever made. I was very backwards and shy growing up and during high school. I came out of the military with much more confidence. Confidence without arrogance is something that will help you immensely in the daily world of police work. Just make sure to keep them balanced.

I clearly recall my third day of U.S. Army Basic Training at Ft Dix, New Jersey. I was truly scared to death. Although Basic Training gets easier as the weeks go on, those first two weeks were pure hell. I remember calling my mom from one of the pay phones and saying, "Mom, I'm coming home". She replied, "No you're not, Brian. Stay there. You'll be fine", and hung up. That was probably the best thing my mother ever did for me. She made me face my fears. My Mom was all about "tough love" and discipline. Because my parents raised me the way they did, my life has been pretty easy. There is no doubt in my mind about that. I think to myself all the time how having good parents was the biggest gift from God that I ever received. Good parents set a foundation. They're a huge influence on how the rest of your life will end up.

Having good parents and a good upbringing really isn't something that you can control. But, you can control your decisions growing up. If you're looking to get into law enforcement, military service, college, and the academy are all things you should highly consider. I did all three, simply because I was going to do everything I possibly could to make myself stick out as a potential candidate. You must set yourself apart from all the other applicants. Like I always tell kids who tell me they want to be police officers, "Don't ever let someone tell you that you can't do it. If you really want it to happen, it will eventually happen".

From the age of eighteen to twenty-five, you can go a lot of different ways in life. As police officers, we deal with those who go the wrong way all too often. Those are the years that you have a lot of energy. Those are the years that you can sleep two hours and bounce out of bed. Don't get me wrong. Those years should be fun, but at the same time, you should be preparing yourself for the rest of your adult life, as well. I took seventeen credit hours at KSU, worked about twenty-five hours a week at Fisher's Foods bagging groceries, and was in the Army National Guard all at the same time. Was it rough? Yes, kind of. But once I graduated from college and started working full-time in law enforcement, life was a breeze. I was suddenly working fifty hours per week, and it honestly felt like a vacation compared to my college years. Everything in life is relative, they say.

The topic often comes up: Does college make you a better police officer? I'd answer that in a very fair and simple way: It certainly does not hurt. I always say that the best police officers are those with a mixture of formal education, real-life experience, and common sense. College helps you in the area of communication skills, builds your confidence, and opens your mind. It tends to make you think for yourself. It makes you a critical thinker. It encourages you to "think outside the box". I'd also argue that when you pay your own way through college, it builds character. It makes you appreciate your education, just like anything else you pay for by yourself.

What about the military? How does that help? Well, there are the obvious ways it helps, and there are some not-so-obvious ways that it helps. Most people are unaware of this, but when you take a civil service exam to be a police officer, you can get bonus points on your exam if you're a veteran of the US Armed Forces (honorably discharged). For example, if you get a passing score of 85%, you'd add a 20% bonus onto your score, and you'd end up with a 102%. Now these rules vary from agency to agency, but as a general rule, that's how it works. In addition, you can "buy" your service credit to apply towards your retirement. For example, in the State of Ohio, you can buy up to five years of military service. Normally, you'd have to work twenty-five years and be forty-eight years of age to retire. Well, if you buy your five years of military service, you'd only have to work twenty years as a police officer to retire. Now one may not be thinking about those things in their twenties, but trust me that you'll be happy you did as you approach retirement age. Good advice was passed onto me when I was a new officer. I always told myself I would do the same for future generations. As I tell people all the time, I have never seen a gravestone that said, "I WISH I WORKED LONGER".

All of these things improve your chances of getting hired, but I always share with those looking into this line of work some motivational thoughts: First and foremost, never let anyone talk you out of it. I hear all the time people telling others to stay away from law enforcement and / or the military. My first thought is: Did the person offering such advice serve in the military or work as a police officer? More often than not, the answer is no. I never really understood that thought process. Why would a person offer advice to someone about something that important when in fact they've never experienced it themselves? Note: Watching "COPS" does not qualify as experience.

A person seeking employment in law enforcement will likely be rejected by many departments before landing a job. It certainly is one of the most difficult positions to get into. Applicants tend to focus on their "dream department". Do not do that. Leave your options open. Apply everywhere. Do Ride-Alongs. Every department is different. They have different contracts, they do different work, they have different budgets, different communities that you serve, different crime trends, etc. When I was applying for positions, I applied all over the State of Ohio. We didn't have the internet back then. I had to use envelopes, stamps, and do a lot of driving. In summary, if you're looking to get into law enforcement, make good choices growing up, but remember that nobody is looking to hire an angel. Do things to make you stick out from the other candidates. Be honest about your shortcomings during the process, and lastly, do not ever let someone talk you out of it or tell you that you cannot do it.

I always tell people, "Nothing worth it is easy. Just keep riding, and you'll see cool things along the way". This is the Old Zoar Bridge located in Zoar, Ohio. A beautiful place...

Chapter Two
"Life Before Police Work"

Like many kids in their mid-teens, I already had life all figured out. Or so I thought. I was focused on joining the police ranks one day. I read books about taking the police exam, even though I could not take the civil service test for another seven years. I knew that all that I could do at that point was prepare myself.

How to do that, I thought? Well, college was not optional. It was mandatory, per my parents. Regardless of my career choice, a college education would have to come first. No questions asked. Logically, my next question would be: How do I pay for it? My job at Fisher's Foods wasn't going to fund a four year degree, so I had to explore other options. One such option was enlisting into the Army National Guard. They offered "free" college tuition, the G.I. Bill, and student loan repayment. Sounded pretty simple to me. I thought that up until the second that that ugly green military bus arrived at US Army Basic Training Reception Station at Ft Dix, NJ. Life as I knew it was about to get real.

I woke up the next morning laying on a military-issue hard steel bunk bed. I was on one of the country's largest U.S. Army bases. I could hear what sounded like drill sergeants in the distance. They were screaming about something. The voices were getting closer and closer. Something told me I was their next victim.

I made the mistake of looking out into the hallway. They had a recruit down knocking out push-ups. Another recruit was at the position of attention, getting ambushed by two drill sergeants at the same time. That poor recruit was getting hammered. I slowly went back into my room, asking myself what I had got myself into this time. "Free college", huh? Yeah, okay.

The next day we would be issued uniforms, gear, get haircuts, and receive multiple shots / vaccinations. Everything was in rapid succession, including your haircut. Nothing says, "Welcome to U.S. Army Basic Training" like your first military haircut. Don't even bother telling them how you like it, because there is only one style: Very short. The first time you look into the mirror and see your ugly bald head, you then realize that life as you know it is no longer. You officially belong to Uncle Sam.

To make it just a little bit worse, anyone wearing contact lenses were issued what the U.S. Army liked to call, "BCDs". Those are the military version of prescription eyewear. BCDs is an acronym for "Birth Control Devices". Once you looked into the mirror and saw how ugly you were, you understood why they called them that.

The first two weeks of basic training were the worst. The drill sergeants pretty much never stopped screaming during that phase. They screamed so much that many of them lost their voices. When they screamed at you, they were so close that you could smell their breath. Little did I know there was a meaning to the madness.

In Phase One, they were covering such things as D&C (Drill & Ceremony), basic military courtesy and customs, rank structure, how to properly wear your uniform, and things like that. Basically, they were teaching you how to carry yourself as a soldier in the United States Army. Many of these very basic things they covered would prove to make me a better person and ultimately help me during a long and challenging law enforcement career.

As the phases went on, the drill sergeants eased up on us slightly. The training became more technical and less psychological. The training became more focused on basic rifle marksmanship, hand-to-hand combat, etc. We completed the obstacle course. We were thrown into the gas chamber. We were slowly becoming soldiers. We had a feeling of accomplishment. It was actually becoming fun to some degree. Well, not really, but it makes for some great stories around the campfire once it's over.

During the final phase of training, we knew graduation was just around the corner. We could smell it. But they had something for us to experience before that day would come. We would be going on a twenty mile forced march thru the sands of Ft Dix, NJ. We would start at 0400 hours and we would not finish the march until around 2200 hours. We would have about fifty pounds of gear on our bodies and we would be carrying our M16A1 rifles at a forty-five degree angle as we marched. Don't let that weapon drop too low. If you did, they'd make an example out of you in front of your platoon members. Again, there was a method to the madness. Everything these drill sergeants did was for a reason. On the other hand, there's no doubt in mind that they'd laugh later behind closed doors. After all, there is nothing more funny than a scared recruit during basic training.

Graduation was approaching soon. It was an amazing feeling. That being said, a few did not make it. I recall seeing one recruit on the back of a pickup truck about half way through basic training. I'll never forget the rejected look on his face as they took him and his gear to out-processing. He was going home. As much as I could not wait to go home, I didn't want to go home like that.

That day finally did come. I recall seeing everyone in their "Class A" uniforms. There was so much pride around there. Graduating from U.S. Army Basic Training was a very proud moment in my life. Although my military service was very limited, it certainly made me much more confident and set a foundation for the rest of my life. It's amazing what military service can do for an individual. I would highly suggest it for anyone looking to get into law enforcement.

After Basic Training came A.I.T. (Advanced Individual Training) at Ft Lee, Va. This was where the U.S. Army taught you your job. I was only going to be here for about four months. Ft Lee was nicknamed "Ft Leisure" because it had a reputation for being a little easier than most training environments. At least that's what I thought.

I was several weeks into A.I.T., and became somewhat relaxed. There were still Drill Sergeants there, but it was not as strict as Basic Training. Although I loved the military life already, I was not a fan of making my bed. As most of you know, there aren't too many things in the military that are optional. Making your bed according to U.S. Army regulations wasn't, either. As I am standing in a company formation one morning, the first sergeant brought it to our attention that a certain member of our company cannot or will not make their bed properly after nine weeks of basic training and four weeks into A.I.T. Something told me that I was the focus of the first sergeant's attention. The next thing I know, a window to the company barracks opens. Out comes pieces and parts of a military bunk. Mattress, sheets, blanket, and then the entire frame hit the ground. I gulped. I knew I was in trouble. I knew it was my bed. They released us, saying that if you return to your quarters and you're missing a bed, come see the first sergeant. I went up to where my bed should have been, and sure enough it was gone. I was very embarrassed. I had failed. It was certainly a low point in my short military life. Nothing is worse than being embarrassed in front of your peers. Needless to say, when everyone else went to Washington, D.C. that weekend, I had CQ duty. Message sent. Message received.

A few weeks later, the first sergeant approached me. He wanted me to run for "Soldier of the Month". I was sort of surprised, seeing that I was the focus of his criticism just a few weeks prior. Still, you didn't say no to the first sergeant. I proudly took on the challenge. I would soon be going in front of a board of veteran NCOs and commissioned officers. They would ask me questions that I better be prepared to answer. I thought to myself: I cannot fail this time. I prepared myself, constantly studying during my time off. One soldier from each platoon would compete, so I was running against three other soldiers. I was later notified by the Lieutenant Colonel (Battalion Commander) that I had won. I couldn't believe it. They presented a trophy to me for "Whiskey Company Soldier of the Month". They did that in front of the entire company of soldiers. I always say that life is full of peaks and valleys. That was a "peak".

Photo: Awarded "Soldier of the Month" at Ft Lee, Va.

I tell that story not to brag, but to explain how the military is very good at breaking you down, and building you back up. Boy, did they do a number on me. As I previously mentioned, in high school and before this point in my life, I was very backwards, and borderline insecure. I suddenly felt much better about myself. The military is very good at making you confident, but also keeping you humble. That would certainly help me during my future police career.

Weeks later, I graduated from A.I.T., and headed back home to the metropolis of Canton South, where I had grown up. I would be assigned to the 107th Armored Cavalry Regiment near the Canton Akron Airport. At that point, I would focus on my college education, as I was still only nineteen years old, and not eligible to work in law enforcement. Per the Ohio Revised Code, any law enforcement officer must be a minimum of twenty-one years of age to be sworn in. Not a problem, I thought. I'll continue to work at Fisher's Foods, bagging groceries, and live the college life while serving in the Army National Guard. My day will come.

Some the best lessons you learn are outside of the classroom, I always say. One such lesson was taught to me while serving in the Army National Guard. I had a battalion commander by the name of Lieutenant Colonel Thomas

Luczynski. I was a Specialist (E-4) when I was assigned to that unit. So needless to say, my contact with an officer of that rank was slim to none. And as a matter of fact, the guy honestly intimidated me, so I avoided him when at all possible. I did watch him from a distance, though. It seemed that he spoke quietly, but everyone obviously respected him. I literally never heard him get angry with any of his troops. I always wondered how he got everyone to follow him like that. I would later figure that out.

Lieutenant Luczynski would eventually reach the rank of Brigadier General before retiring from the Army National Guard. That is quite an accomplishment. You do not reach that rank by accident. I am convinced that a large part of how he reached that rank was by treating people with respect. He also led by example, and still does. I know that because we ran into each other years later during my law enforcement career. We often have coffee together. He's a good man. Crossing paths with people like that in your life are true blessings.

Photo: Army National Guard General Thomas Luczynski

I had to continue focusing on graduating from college. I wanted nothing to do with police work, until I had that degree on paper. I took seventeen credit hours while working twenty-five hours per week at Fisher's Foods and fulfilling my military obligations. Life was stressful, but it went by very quickly. I would watch some of the students wasting time every day. I often wondered if they ever went to class. Every time I saw them, they were in the student lounge playing cards, laughing away. What a life, I thought.

Classes were challenging. Some more than others. I remember thinking that my best professors were those with former law enforcement experience. You could always tell the difference between a professor with no practical experience and one who spent time in the field. I wasn't the only one who noticed that, either. It was blatantly obvious. I am of the opinion that your best applicant has both a formal education as well as some real-world experience. They both help you, immensely during your career.

I didn't attend the main campus of Kent State University until my senior year of college, and it's probably a good thing, because it's easy to get distracted there. That's saying it lightly. Although I was never really much of a drinker, I did have my moments. One such night, I was walking home from one of Kent's many college bars, and could not seem to find my dorm. I walked and walked and walked. Eventually, I gave up. I found a tree and laid down under it, trying to get my bearings. Next thing I know, I woke up to the sun rising, dew on my face. Students were walking by on their way to classes, laughing at me. Chalk up another proud moment in my life.

My roommate and I decided to have a party in our KSU dorm one evening. Alcohol was obviously involved. During this little get-together, someone called campus security on us. They were called because something was seen hanging from my sixth story dorm window. Their investigation led them find cans of Bud Light inside of a potato sack hanging from the window sill. I explained to them that I could not afford a fridge, so I would hang it out of the window during the winter months to stay nice and cool. I don't think they were impressed with my invention. Neither was my background investigator who would later run across that tidbit of information as he looked into my life history. Yep. Those things tend to pop up either before or during your long police career. Again, cops aren't angels. They have good days and bad days. They make good decisions and bad ones. They're human beings just like you.

Graduation from KSU would soon come shortly thereafter. Finally, it seemed. Everything was coming together. I was ready to have a "normal life". No more juggling a schedule. No more surviving on Ramen Noodles. Little did I know that life as a cop would be anything but normal.

But, before I would reach the police ranks, I first had to go thru the rigorous hiring process. Getting a job as a law enforcement officer is a challenge in and of itself. Unlike most civilian positions, you must first take a civil service examination. They only offer these exams once a year at the most, and each agency has their own test, so you can quickly understand how it can become a full-time just getting hired on.

I always would encourage those interested in a law enforcement career to join the military during those years from eighteen to twenty-one. Most states have a minimum age requirement of twenty-one anyways, so serving your country during that "down time" is time well spent, so to say. There are numerous reasons to serve in the military prior to a law enforcement career. First and foremost, it lays a foundation for your entire life. You'll learn things in the military that you could never learn in a classroom anywhere. In addition, when you take the civil service exam, more often than not, you get "bonus points" on your exam for serving in the military. Those bonus points are normally twenty percent of your passing grade, and can be a game-changer during the employment process.

Another reason to consider serving your country before becoming a law enforcement officer isn't so obvious. Most applicants are not thinking about retirement when they're looking to get into law enforcement, but the earlier you can get out of law enforcement with all of your limbs attached and your mind somewhat straight, the better off you are. In most police pension systems, you can "buy" your military service up to five years. Costs vary, but the earlier you buy it, the cheaper it is. For example, I purchased 1.2 years of military service for about $5,000. That's a no-brainer. Time on Planet Earth obviously is invaluable, for one. Secondly, you'll collect much more than it cost you to purchase it. Not to mention, you're not out in the elements chasing drunks at 3am any longer. Instead, you'll be inside of a warm donut shop with your laptop, writing a book.

Getting back to the hiring process, it was anything but easy. I took civil service exams all over the State of Ohio. We didn't have the internet when I was job-searching in the early '90's. I had to use envelopes, stamps, and drive around the state. Each test was slightly different. Most tested "common knowledge". I took exams for Dublin, Canton, Ohio State Highway Patrol, Kent, Ritman, and Massillon. As they announced an exam, I signed up and took them. I really wanted to work in the county I grew up in (Stark County), but I would have accepted a position anywhere.

Eventually, Massillon Police Department sent me a letter. They said that I had passed the civil service exam, and would go onto the next phase of the process. That would be the physical agility. It was similar to a physical training test in the military, so I wasn't too concerned. Your basic two mile run, pushups and situps. I passed that with flying colors.

Next step was the background investigation. In this step, they go deep into your life history, looking for any potential patterns of misconduct that may disqualify you, or any patterns of behavior that may be a "red flag" to an investigator. Such red flags are bad credit, abuse of alcohol / drugs, violent behavior, sloppy living conditions, etc. Disqualifiers would be such things as OVI convictions, a suspended driver's license, a domestic violence conviction, or other obvious things that show up during the earliest stages of a background investigation.

Detective Bobby Grizzard (Retired) did my background investigation. He talked to a lot of people about me. One of those people was my current roommate at the time. He asked my roommate the following question: What's the worst thing about Brian that you can tell me? My roommate answered, "Well, he sure does eat a lot of chips". Yes, we all have vices, and one of mine was chips. To this day, I cannot stay away from them. And I tend to eat the entire bag. Of course it ended up as part of my personnel file. My obsession with potato chips was now a matter of public record. My mother had to be so proud.

Photo: MPD Detective Bobby Grizzard

Some departments utilize polygraph examinations during their process. I took one during my application process for the Ohio State Highway Patrol. To put it lightly, I probably looked like the guy on "Meet the Parents" when I sat thru those three grueling hours of very uncomfortable questions. Yeah, they're no fun. We've all done things we're not so proud of. Just tell the truth. Again, we're not looking for angels.

Part of the interview process was being interviewed by a board of individuals. The board was made up of the Chief of Police, the Safety Director, and an individual from the EEOC. This formal interview was obviously a very crucial. I recall two very specific questions they asked. The first question they asked me was worded as such: "We see you're from Canton South. Being a predominantly white community, how will you deal with people of a lower socio-economic background and/or minorities?" I answered by saying if I told them I'd treat everyone the same, I'd be lying. I'm not a robot and either are those I'd be serving. I think what you want to concentrate on is treating everyone with respect and treating them fairly. But remember to do your job, regardless of anything else.

The second question asked was if I would write my own mother a ticket. I thought about it for a split second and replied, "No I would not. My mother brought me into this world and she would take me out of it just as fast". Although they appeared surprised by my answer, I think they appreciated my honesty.

Photo: My parents just after they qualified to get their Concealed Carry permits. They were by far the greatest gift I ever received.

After taking and somehow passing the psychological exam portion of the hiring process, I eventually received what's called a "conditional offer of employment". I was hired on the condition that I pass the last portion of the process, a medical examination. After that very thorough physical exam, I eventually got a call from Chief Mark Weldon. I was officially hired, and would be swearing in with the mayor in a couple weeks.

At that point, I had to pause and take this all in. Everything that I had done up to this point in my life was actually paying off. I was going to become a full-time police officer in the second largest city in Stark County. Little did I know, my life was about to change in so many ways.

Photo: I would catch myself looking at the night skies during my career, looking for answers. As a cop, I'd soon learn that the world is a crazy place.

Chapter 3
"Life as a Rookie"

There I was in the mayor's office, waiting to swear in as a police officer. I was nervous, hoping that I wouldn't mess up my oath of office. The mayor had me raise my hand and repeat after him.

"I do solemnly swear that I will support the Constitution of the United States of America, the Constitution and Laws of the State of Ohio, the Laws and Ordinances of the City of Massillon, and the Rules and Regulations of the Massillon Police Department, and that I will faithfully discharge the duties of Police Officer in the City of Massillon, which I have been appointed according to law and to the best of my ability, so help me God".

Somehow, I got through it without screwing it up and embarrassing myself before I even clocked in. I thought about the end of that oath. I thought about how God had put me in this position in my life, and that he gave me powers that most people do not have. He gave me the authority to make warrantless misdemeanor arrests. He gave me the authority to take someone's life in the event I had to in order to protect myself or someone else from serious physical harm or death. On the other hand, I thought about how along with power goes responsibility. I thought about how I could not fail God. He trusted me like he trusts others in positions of authority. We must take that responsibility seriously. We mustn't let Him down.

If you ever have the opportunity to swear in as a police officer, public official, or into the U.S. Armed Forces, the swearing in ceremony is usually a very cool experience. It really makes you think about what responsibilities you're taking on. I'd suggest that you take friends and/or family members with you. Have a decent photographer there. It's a moment you should document forever.

Photo: Mike Maier swearing in as a lieutenant as his family watches.

Once the administrative stuff was out of the way, it was time to go to work. My first day as a uniformed police officer on road patrol was about to happen. My first shift would be on afternoon shift. That's the busiest shift on the department, and is similar at most law enforcement agencies around the country.

Walking towards the police department for the first time, I looked like a textbook rookie. I had every piece of police equipment known to mankind on my duty belt. I literally had a PR-24 side baton hanging from my waist, and I hadn't even clocked in. There were a group of uniformed officers hanging around by the rear entrance to the police department. They were watching me approach the building, sizing me up. As I got near the back door, a guy in civilian clothes stopped me. He sounded very angry and impatient to say the least and he was speaking to me in this ridiculous sounding voice that was nearly making me laugh. Needless to say, it was very difficult to make out what he was saying. He said at least three times, "Do you know where da cour-houth is?". After the third time I asked him to repeat himself, he screams, "You mean to tell me yer a polithe-man and you don' know where da cour-houth is??!!". I did not want to insult the man about his speech, so instead I looked over his shoulders to the uniformed officers for their help in translating the man's words. I eventually realized that he was looking for the courthouse. He then spoke normally, and introduced himself as the retiring officer who I was replacing. All I could think was how I had not even clocked in yet, and they already got me good.

That was my first test, and I passed with flying colors. They got a good laugh out of me, and I didn't take it personal. Now it was time to meet with the Chief of Police, Field Training Officers, and my fellow officers. Officer Kenny Hendricks was a true veteran. He had been around the block, so to say. He had salt and pepper hair. He liked to talk a lot and always had an opinion, but he could back it up both physically and mentally. He knew his stuff when it came to police work. On the other hand, he was a jokester, and had great "people skills". I would watch him talk to people. Although he was physically intimidating, he knew how to talk to people, and that kept him out of trouble.

I was watching my FTO's every move. I was taking it all in. One of the things I learned from him was about how to use your mouth instead of your body. Treating people with respect and de-escalating a situation often will keep you out of situations you don't want to be in. Don't get me wrong. Some people only understand one thing: Bracelets on their wrists. That is a fact, too. I learned these things quickly during my field training.

Photo: My first Field Training Officer (Detective Kenny Hendricks)

I recall one comical time during my first four weeks of field training. I was in a foot pursuit on the southeast side of the city. Knowing your location during a pursuit is crucial for obvious reasons. Growing up in Canton South, the only street I knew in Massillon was Lincoln Way. The only reason I knew that street was because we cruised the strip constantly looking for trouble during my late teens. As I was chasing the suspect thru alleys and neighborhoods, I hear dispatch calling me asking for my location. Knowing I had no clue where I was other than "Massillon", I just kept chasing him, and didn't answer. I was getting winded and with the weight of all my gear, the chase was wearing me down. Luckily, he tripped and I basically landed on top of him. Dispatch was repeatedly asking me for my location. I asked the suspect what his address was, as we were only a few hundred feet from his home. Surprisingly, he told me. I got on the radio, breathing heavily, and gave the suspect's address. Little did anyone know that the reason I wasn't answering the dispatcher had nothing to do with me being out of breath. I simply had absolutely no idea where I was. That was a lesson to me to get a better grasp of my geography. My life (or others' lives) could depend on it. I got lucky that time.

As field training went on, I was feeling more and more confident. My FTOs would sit back and let me be the primary contact officer. The only problem with that training theory was that I had a baby-face, and citizens would naturally go directly towards the veteran officer for help. I recall one evening when a drunk I had arrested repeatedly said that there was no way I could be a cop and that I was too young to take him to jail. After about the tenth time he said that, I looked up from the booking desk as I typed, and said, "Sir. Apparently you're wrong, because you're

currently sitting in jail, and I am typing up your arrest report."
That conversation was over. Rookie 1, Bad Guy 0.

Photo: My D.A.R.E. card (Rookie Edition)

As I continued onto midnight shift phase of my training, the
type of calls for service would change. I quickly learned that
people act differently after midnight. They're less likely to
cooperate with you, and alcohol / drugs become a huge

factor in their decision-making. I recall being in the car with Sgt JJ DiLoreto (Retired). He was driving and I was just along for the ride. It was my first few nights with Sgt DiLoreto, and that's par for the course before your FTO allows you to actually drive the car with them in it. We attempted to stop a car on suspicion that the driver was impaired, and it was immediately apparent that the suspect was not going to stop. He took us thr several neighborhoods on the NE side. That my first actual pursuit. When someone runs from you for the first time, your immediate thoughts become that of disbelief. How dare someone not stop for the police? Pursuits are extremely dangerous. They're actually one of the most dangerous things you'll encounter in police work. I saw my share of them during my career. They never ended good. Some worse than others.

You don't remember everything your FTOs teaches you, but you certainly take a lot in from them. I remember when Sgt DiLoreto once told me, "Brian, looking good is half the job". I asked him what he meant by that. He explained that career criminals will size you up. They'll judge you based on how you wear your uniform, whether you look them in the eye when you speak to them, if your cruiser is clean and maintained. First impressions are important. Especially in police work. Sgt DiLoreto was a wealth of knowledge. I was very thankful for my FTO's experience and patience with Massillon's newest rookie.

Photo: J.J. DiLoreto (retired MPD Sergeant)

Field training was twelve weeks long. Once those twelve weeks were over, and your FTOs signed off on your training, you would be assigned to a shift and be placed on "solo patrol". I successfully passed field training, and would be assigned to afternoon shift. Afternoon shift was by far the busiest shift on the department. It was entirely normal to get between forty and sixty calls for service between 2pm and 10pm. The nice thing about working afternoons as a rookie is that you tend to get a wide variety of calls, so you learn quickly. Everything including crashes (lots of them), shoplifters, domestics, assaults, robberies, theft, fraud, suspicious persons, felonious assault, murder, you name it.

Some calls are more dangerous than others, obviously. I recall one afternoon during my first few years, where they sent a few cars to look for a subject with a hand grenade. Immediately when I heard the radio call go out, I thought to myself that perhaps I had taken a wrong turn in life. Regardless, now wasn't the time to reflect on my decisions. I had a job to do. As I arrived on scene, the entire shift arrived with me. That's the nice thing about being a city police officer. Your backup gets there quickly. Every single time. We found the suspect holding a device in his hand, saying that it was a grenade and that he pulled the "pin". One of the officers was able to wrestle the device from his hands, and threw it over a fence. It exploded shortly thereafter, and he was arrested without any injuries to the officers on scene. We would later learn that it was actually a military training device (an artillery simulator). Regardless what it was, I was pretty sure I was going to die that day. Although it took a nice-sized hole out of the concrete, none of us were injured. God had other plans.

I was quickly learning that this job was extremely dangerous and that anything can happen anywhere at anytime. Calls like the aforementioned tended to remind you how dangerous it actually was. As a police officer, you tend to have a false sense of security. What's normal to you isn't normal to everyone else. What frightens others doesn't frighten you. Only because your average day is slightly different from a someone not serving in law enforcement. Not to mention, you're carrying a 9mm with forty-plus rounds and wearing a bullet-proof vest. But, I suppose that's also healthy for the mind, as well. You can't obsess over what can happen every day. When it happens, you just do what you have to do. Don't worry about the Monday morning quarterbacks. They'll always do their thing. They are who they are and you you are who you are. Just remember: They weren't there. They did not experience what you did on that call. And that includes other cops who were not on scene. End of story.

Photo: MPD officers before our annual Memorial Day detail (mid-1990's).

Like many rookie officers, I loved traffic enforcement. The reason I enjoyed it was because I knew that as long as I had "reasonable articulable suspicion" for the stop, it often led to bigger things. You'd find them to be unlicensed, impaired (alcohol and/or drugs), and they often had warrants. All because I noticed something minor like failing to signal a turn, a license plate light out, or they failed to display a front plate. If they were "clean", I'd let them go with a warning, and go "fishing" again. Most cops do it at one point or another during their career, and it's completely legal (and rightfully so). Some will complain and call it "harassment". My answer? Start using your turn signal, put a front plate on your car, get your license reinstated, take care of your warrants, and you'll never get "harassed" again. Onward.

Often people ask, "When is a rookie no longer a rookie? I tell them that there are two rules about being a rookie. First and foremost, anyone with less time in law enforcement than you is a rookie. Secondly, you stop being a rookie when you stop acting like one. That's the easiest way to define the label that nobody wants to wear.

You'll quickly learn that there are certain veteran officers whom you can never satisfy. No matter what you do, they did it better. No matter what you did, they would have done it differently. Although they can certainly get on your nerves at times, remember that they likely know more than you do at that point in your career. Even if their delivery isn't the greatest, tip your hat to them, learn from them, and hope that your delivery is better than theirs when it's your turn to wear the veteran hat.

Remember that as you work your way up the corporate ladder of the law enforcement world, you're building a reputation. Your reputation as a law enforcement officer is of utmost importance. Are you trustworthy or are you a liar? A liar is no good on a witness stand. You can quickly understand how honesty is an important attribute as a police officer. Trust me that you will make mistakes. You will make bad choices. But remember to be honest about whatever you do. Most supervisors and the citizens whom you serve can understand a lapse in judgment. On the other hand, police work has no room for liars. Keep that in mind if you end up wearing the uniform one day.

Photo: MPD Patrolman's badge

As the first couple rookie years went on, the job became easier, and much more fun. One of things I enjoyed most about police work was that I didn't have anyone staring over my shoulder all the time. I was pretty much my own boss, making my own decisions on the streets. One thing I learned quickly was to know the Ohio Revised Code. The Ohio Revised Code (O.R.C.) is a law officer's Bible. You don't have to know it word for word, but there are certain laws that you should have a very good grasp of, because you'll have to make quick decisions in regards to whether someone is violation of the code or not. One of my FTOs gave me some very good advice one day. He said, "If you don't know, don't do." In other words, you're better off walking away from a situation and getting an arrest warrant later than to make a "bad arrest". Nobody wants to be sued for false arrest. Again, some good advice from Sgt J.J. DiLoreto.

If there was anything I learned my first few years that really stuck out in my mind, it would be to listen to your veteran officers. They've seen things that you haven't. They're an invaluable asset to a law enforcement agency.

That is something that Chief Robert Williams always told me. He was a really good guy, and a great chief. He would tell officers when they did something good, and he would also tell you when you messed up. I respected him for that. I took on some great advice from Chief Robert Williams during the midst of my career when I needed guidance. God Bless you, Chief. Hope you're enjoying retirement.

Photo: Chief Robert Williams (Retired)

Chapter 4
"Midnights"

After a few years on afternoon shift as a rookie, I was able to go to midnight shift. I had a few years under my belt, and just enough experience to get myself into trouble. The city looked different at night. The people you'd be dealing with were not the same, and almost all of them were impaired by either alcohol or drugs, and often both.

Knowing that I would be dealing with "drunks", I put in for a class related to DUI enforcement. In the 1990's, it was called, "D.U.I." which stood for Driving Under the Influence. It later became "O.V.I.", which stands for Operating a Vehicle Impaired". In essence, they're the same thing. Don't ask me why they changed the terminology. It confused everyone, including the cops. The only explanation I can give you is that that's what happens when the world has too many attorneys.

Being a police officer on midnight shift in a city environment was no walk in the park. Usually, calls for service were waiting when you got to work. Roll-call was usually pretty quick, and you were handling calls immediately, especially on the weekend. Most calls were "two-man calls" simply because of the danger involved. The most common calls were suspicious persons / vehicles, fights, disturbances, domestics, robbery, burglary, breaking and entering, you name it. Crashes were not as often, but when you did get them, they usually were hit-skips and / or OVI crashes, and often were accompanied by serious injuries. I was quickly learning how cruel the world could be.

Photo: Sgt Tom Rogers and Sgt Kenny Smith in a two-man car on midnights.

Although the types of calls were dangerous and serious in nature, I was also learning my new profession very quickly. As I've said before, I am a slow learner. It took me repetition to learn new tasks. That wasn't an issue, though. Reason being, the calls never stopped. And often they were the same exact things, often the same players.

Nights are for working

By BRIGETTE BARNES
Independent Staff Writer

As most Massillonians settle down for the night, a few are just getting up and getting ready for work.

Bakers, doctors, nurses and police are just a few occupations of those on the night shift.

And working while others are sleeping can be stressful, both personally and professionally.

Shelley Gray, charge nurse in the emergency department at Massillon Community Hospital, said most night workers are isolated from the hospital staff.

"You don't see managers and supervisors who work during the day," she said, adding when she is required to come to a meeting at the hospital, it is on her off time in the morning, which usually is set aside for sleeping.

Despite the challenges, most people who work the night shift say they enjoy it, as long as they can stay on one schedule and don't have to keep switching back and forth from night to day.

Gray said she actually enjoys working during the night better than during the day.

"It's a closer knit unit," she said, noting fewer personnel work in the emergency room during the night shift. "You rely on each other more."

According to "Emergency Nursing World," a Web site designed especially for emergency

Please see NIGHT SHIFT, Page A-5

Photo: "The Inde" did an article on midnight shift workers while I was assigned to the graveyard shift (Photo credit: The Massillon Independent).

I recall one injury OVI crash I handled early in my career. A suspected OVI driver had blown a stop sign and struck a minivan broadside. The minivan was hit so hard that it careened off at a forty-five degree angle and ran into a house. A fifteen year old boy suffered a serious injury to his jaw during the crash. I recall the young boy being worried about what girls would think about his appearance. Seeing that young boy in pain, worried about his future social life was all the motivation I needed to go after OVI drivers the rest of my career.

Going after drunks was on my mind every time I sat in that cruiser. I'd do a quick equipment check on the radar, emergency lights, spotlight, siren, check the back seat for drug paraphernalia, and I was on the hunt. I knew they were out there, especially on midnights. And I was determined to get a few off the streets every night. There were nights when you could not do that because of call volume, but as a general rule, that was the plan.

Drunks were so easy. If they only knew how bad they stuck out like to an officer trained in "A.D.A.P." A.D.A.P. stood for Advanced Detection Apprehension and Prosecution of OVI offenders. I'd look for clues such as no turn signal, making a wide right turn, slow response to a green light. Then there were the more obvious clues like speed, left of center, etc. Often you'd pull up behind a car at 2:30am at a red light. As soon as you'd pull up behind them, they'd do one of two things. They'd either throw a half-used cigarette butt out the window (because of nervousness), or they'd suddenly put on their right turn signal, and turn. Poor choices, because both are illegal, and that gave me a reason to stop them and see if they were impaired, unlicensed, had warrants, or all the above. Littering from a motor vehicle is obviously a violation and when you make a turn or lane change, a signal must be used no less than one hundred feet prior to the change of direction (ORC section 4511.39). That's where knowing the O.R.C. paid off during my career. Knowing your laws and paying attention to people's mannerisms were extremely important while on patrol.

I recall one traffic stop that sticks out in my head to this day. Like I said, I was really into going after OVI / DUI drivers. I stopped a car in the 500 block of Lincoln Way East, and they pulled into Wendy's. Before pulling all the way into the lot, the driver and front seat passenger switched spots. I figured one was more drunk than the other. I was right. I ended up arresting them both for OVI, but then it got worse. As I was doing an inventory on the vehicle in the parking lot, a second vehicle pulled up and sat behind my cruiser and the driver was staring, looking confused, staring at my emergency lights. I walked up to his driver's side. He was nearly passed out at the wheel. I ordered him out, and arrested him, too. One traffic stop. Three OVI arrests. I've never heard of that happening anywhere before. Lt Witmer pulled up after hearing me ask for two tow trucks and advising three OVI arrests on the radio. He looked at me, laughed, and said, "You're outta control". I told him that my mom tells me the same thing. I guess I was. But hey. I had another story to tell, right?

Photo: Lt Donald Witmer. We all miss him. God Bless you, Lieutenant.

Along with traffic enforcement went other things, simply because you'd come into contact with so many people on traffic stops. Saying that drug enforcement wasn't a strength of mine is an understatement. That being said, I always say that the most intelligent people know what they don't know. And they surround themselves with others who know what they don't. "Relationships are Opportunities", my brother Dennis would always say. Having good working relationships with your coworkers paid off. I knew Lieutenant Jason Greenfield was very knowledgeable of the drug laws. He was only a phone call away, and was always eager to help when I ran across something that reminded me how much I did not know. My knowledge of drugs was once summed up by Cpt Paul Covert. He said, "Here's Munster speaking in regards to drugs: "DRUGS: BAD." That pretty much summed it up. Thanks, Cap. Oh well, I knew my strengths and weaknesses. Onward.

Along with midnights came pursuits. Lots of them. Pursuits are one of the most dangerous things in a law enforcement officer's career. They're very unpredictable. They taught us in emergency driving courses to "drive at seventy percent of your abilities". They teach you to leave thirty percent for driver error, equipment failure, and other "unknowns" that can and often do occur during a vehicle pursuit. During a pursuit, you're making many decisions, and you're making them quickly. You're constantly trying to gauge if the reason for the pursuit is justified, based on the speed, traffic conditions, weather conditions, etc. Of course, you have meer seconds to think about it. Those who judge your decisions after the fact have the luxury of time.

The trend I saw in regards to police pursuits is for everyone to question the choices of the officer after the fact. Then you have police administrators who completely ban pursuits unless they're chasing a quadruple murder suspect. At what point don't we (as a society) question the choices of the person running from the police? At what point don't we have mandatory minimum sentencing for those who make the choice to run from the police? If you have department policies banning vehicle pursuits, and combine that with the fact that we have no mandatory minimum sentencing, the criminal element is more likely to run from the police. And they often do. Logic being that there is a chance they'll get away and never be identified. And even if they are identified, they're likely to plea bargain it down to a misdemeanor with a half decent attorney at their side. It's a win-win scenario for them. I've seen it far too many times.

I recall one pursuit very clearly. I was on midnights. Like many cops, I was working a "double". I was about twelve hours into my sixteen hour tour. The radio was uncomfortably quiet. I was enjoying some rare peace and serenity, but something told me it wouldn't last long. Suddenly, I hear an officer on the radio, advising he was in pursuit of our own police department's prisoner van. The vehicle had apparently been stolen from the fenced-in street department facility, and rammed through the fence on the way out. The suspect had already struck one motorist who was stopped at a stoplight on the city's southwest side. The veteran officer was in pursuit, calling out his location and direction of travel, lights and siren blaring in the background. "Wonderful", I thought. The pursuit continued for about five to eight minutes. At one point, I was about the second or third police vehicle in the pursuit as it went down a curvy road on the city's southeast side. The fog was thick that evening, and suddenly the suspect lost control of the van, going through two utility poles, eventually wrapping the van around a huge oak tree. Both poles came crashing down to the ground, high power lines were now all around me. Of course, the suspect was able to get out and run on foot after all of that. I got out, giving chase, and during the foot pursuit, lost one of my boots in some thick mud. Now I was chasing him, wearing one boot, running through thorns. Thankfully, my fellow officers caught up to him and cuffed him. That was one of those moments when you wonder where you went wrong in life since you're running thru the woods with one boot on at 3am.

Police pursuits are often glorified by video games and by Hollywood. In reality, they're extremely dangerous, and often lead to serious injury or death. The average person does not look at it that way until one of their loved ones are struck and killed or paralyzed from the waist down by someone who thought running from the police was a good idea. Running from the police is a choice and a very selfish choice, I'll add. I've been in many pursuits during my career, and they often do not end well. I watched people die under the light of the moon because of choices that they made. Society should focus their attention on the bad guys' behavior, not the good guys' behavior. I'll leave it at that.

Don't get me wrong. As human beings, we all make mistakes. All of us. But what rubs me the wrong way is how this country coddles repeat offenders. A prime example is repeat OVI offenders. It was not uncommon for us to run across someone with five to ten prior convictions for OVI. Some had actual valid driver's licenses. You'd ask yourself how that is possible in the United States of America? Well, under Ohio law, one must have either four OVIs in six years or six OVIs in twenty years before it's a felony. NHTSA statistics estimate that in the United States, the average OVI driver only gets arrested once every ninety-seven times they commit the offense. If you "do the math", you'll understand how that's possible. You can have ten OVI convictions, but if they're over a twenty-five year period, then they're only charged with a misdemeanor. The laws certainly need to be strengthened. Say what you want, but there is no way someone with ten OVIs should be walking around in society, free as a bird. People often say, "Take away their car", or "take away their plates". Trust me that they already do that. They find cars to drive. They steal license plates. They date women with cars so they can drive their car around. They do whatever they have to do to drive. They're given every chance at "help" by the courts that you think of. They continue to drive drunk. Like I've said numerous times; There are only two things that'll stop some repeat offenders from driving drunk again. A prison cell, or a casket.

Any officer assigned to midnight shift is going to respond to their fair share of domestic violence calls. Sadly, they're extremely common. They're also extremely dangerous. To understand why they're so dangerous, you have to look at what factors are present in most domestic violence calls. First and foremost, most domestics occur in the home. Along with someone's home often goes firearms or other weapons, even if it's a kitchen knife or other blunt object. Secondly, along with relationships go emotions. Emotions make people do things that they normally wouldn't do. Then you add alcohol and/or drugs to the equation, which makes it even worse. When you combine emotions, access to firearms, and alcohol / drugs, you have the potential for things to go very wrong. And they often do.

Domestics are one of the most frustrating types of calls in police work. The law in Ohio puts pressure on law enforcement to make an arrest if probable cause exists to do so. It doesn't say that we have to make an arrest, but it does say that the preferred action is to arrest the "primary aggressor". It also says that if we do not make an arrest, we must file a police report indicating why we chose not to. To put that in perspective, no other criminal offense (including murder) in the Ohio Revised Code puts that type of responsibility on the responding officer.

Often, we respond to a domestic disturbance call and the victim is uncooperative. He / she will tell us that they fell down the steps when asked about their obvious injuries. They'll hide the offender in the house, and lie to us about their whereabouts. They'll insist that the offender doesn't go to jail and ask that you just "tell them to leave". It's like they want you to referee their boxing match. Add alcohol to the equation and it gets even worse. If you leave them there together, you just know dispatch is going to call you on the radio within the hour and send you back to that same address.

Even when you do make the arrest, often the victim won't show up for court to testify. If they do show up for court, they'll change their story. Documentation via photographs and body-cam video becomes extremely important in domestic violence calls simply because often you cannot rely on testimony from the victims. Many times I have asked a domestic violence victim why they are still living with the offender, knowing we've been there numerous times for domestics. They'll look you square in the eye and say, "Because I love him". It's a vicious cycle that after serving twenty-five years, I still don't understand. I've heard theories about it from people with numerous initials behind their name and multiple degrees on their "love-me wall", but it's very obvious that they've never walked in the shoes of a police officer.

Officers who work midnights for an extended period of time are a different breed. I spent half of my career assigned that shift. I mean, think about it. While the rest of the world is either partying or sleeping, you're dealing with the worst of society on their worst day. On the other hand, it can be very peaceful, especially on a Sunday night in the middle of winter. But if you're on patrol, and it seems a little too quiet, get ready because it can change really quick. And it often does. You see things that change you forever. I always felt bad for the rookie officer who never saw a dead person. I mean, like they never even saw one at a funeral. Next thing they know, they're on a nasty suicide or homicide, and you can see the look in their eyes. I'd usually take a hard look at them while on scene, and think about how they'll never be the same.

Midnights can be rough. Like I said before, they can literally take years off of your life. But they give you a wealth of experience and you'll have stories to tell around the campfire for the rest of your life.

Photo: Sgt Jason McCune, Officer Kervin Brown, Detective Kenny Hendricks, Sgt Tom Rogers, Detective Nevada Gump, Cpt Joe Herrick, and Lt Jason Greenfield. They went to Washington, DC for "Police Week" to honor fallen MPD Officer Eric Taylor and the tens of thousands of law enforcement officers in this country who gave "The Ultimate Sacrifice".

Chapter Five
"Off-Duty"

Being a single cop in your mid-twenties, you can easily get into trouble. There are way too many distractions and temptations. I would often tell people I have no idea how I survived my career. Especially the first ten years of it. I would always tell rookie officers that there are two things that'll destroy a police career more often than anything else; Alcohol and women. Thankfully, my fellow officers knew me as "Two-Beer Brian", since I couldn't drink more than two beers. And women were never a problem simply because I was too ugly for that to ever become a major issue.

The first thing you notice about your off-duty life is that some of your friends, family, and associates see life differently than you. Not all of them, but some of them. Especially when you try to explain the reality of police work to them. Simply put, their version of reality is no longer the same as yours. You see things that they do not. And you see them on a consistent basis. Your life experiences are no longer the same as the vast majority of the public. That can certainly become a problem in your personal life if you allow it to.

It's no secret that police work can be rough on a marriage. Or at least you'd think that from what you hear and read. The truth of the matter is that there is no research to back that up. In fact, most research puts the divorce rate of police officers below the national average when comparing divorce rates strictly by profession.

On the other hand, police work certainly can be challenging when it comes to mixing it with a marriage or any relationship for that matter. Let's face it. Cops are cynical. They tend to have egos. They tend to want control of any situation. I'm not speaking badly about them. I am one. It's just reality. If you didn't possess some of those traits, you likely would not perform well in law enforcement. Police work can be nasty at times. In order to bring order to chaos, you better have somewhat of an ego.

I would often hear that stress was what causes divorces to those in the police ranks. I disagree. There are many stressful jobs out there. I believe there are many things about police work that can cause dysfunction in a relationship. I always tell people that "Knowledge is Power". The more you know about what you're about to get into, the more likely you'll survive your career.

I jokingly tell people that in police work, you have to get divorced before you get promoted. It's like a right of passage. I was one of the many law enforcement "statistics". Nobody bats 1.000 in life, and I was no exception. Two marriages, two divorces. The first one was certainly due to my immaturity. I was thirty years old, and thought that marriage was what you were supposed to do. That's what society expected me to do, so I did it. She was a wonderful girl, very goal oriented. She was focused on her career and I was focused on everything but being married. That relationship had no chance of surviving. Five years later, she filed for divorce. Years later, I would find myself apologizing to her for being so inconsiderate and selfish. She deserved better than that. Thankfully, she got happily remarried.

You'd often hear people blame "stress" on marriage problems and infidelity. I never really agreed with that theory. I actually didn't think police work was that stressful. At least as a patrol officer. I felt that there were other factors that led to relationship problems. I always would tell people that if you had all your teeth and half of a personality, it was very easy to meet women. For whatever reason, they certainly loved that uniform. In addition, you were almost always on your own, unsupervised for the most part. Of course if you were dedicated to your marriage, those factors weren't an issue. If you had issues in your marriage and/or were not happy, then you can see how the odds were stacked against you.

I rode motorcycles when I was off-duty. I rode sport bikes, and we all know what they're made for. Zero to sixty. I was honestly fortunate to live through those years. Like many young males in their twenties and thirties, I thought I was invincible. Although I never mixed alcohol with any of those activities, my love for speed and acceleration very easily could have led to a disaster. God was on my side, as luckily that never happened.

My Honda RC51. Glad I survived those days...

Point being, it's not anything I am proud of, but I want to point out that cops are regular people who have temptations and from time to time do things that they should not be doing. You just hope and pray that you can make it through those vulnerable years with only a few scars. They're very dangerous times. You're mixing the responsibilities of being a police officer with living the life of a young adult when you're supposed to be having fun. You can easily understand how bad things can happen.

Shift work can be rough on family life, too. Working midnights means you're not in bed until 6:30am at the earliest. No matter how long you're on them, the rest of the world forgets. Or they simply don't care about the fact that you were wrestling with a drunk at 3am while they were asleep like most normal people. One thing I quickly realized is the rest of the world has no interest in adapting to the life of a vampire.

Social situations could be a little awkward as an off-duty cop. For whatever reason, your friends would introduce you like this; "This is Brian….he's a police officer." I'd always cringe when people would do that for a few different reasons. For one, I have no idea what the person I was being introduced to thought of law enforcement. Perhaps they just got arrested the week prior. Maybe they had warrants. Maybe they just committed a double homicide. Secondly, I'm a person. Being a police officer was usually not relevant to the social situation that I was in, and at times, it would make people uncomfortable (for a variety of reasons).

I recall being invited to a party one night by a long-time friend of mine. Once I got there, I started wondering who owned the glamorous home that we were in. It was highly unlikely that a bunch of young adults in their early twenties owned the place. Things weren't adding up. I also recall getting a very weird vibe from some people there who knew I was a cop. I was pretty sure some of the people there were drinking underage. My gut instinct told me that I needed to leave. I took my friend to the side and told him I did not feel comfortable being there for a multitude of reasons. I also asked him to use better judgement in the future when involving me in some of these activities. I think he may have been somewhat offended, but I knew the difference between right and wrong, and that was not how I was raised. I left and I felt good about that decision. I recall thinking to myself how my life changed because of my career choice. Even though I was off-duty, if something bad happened, I knew I would be judged by others as a police officer, not as a civilian. That was a learning moment for me early in my career.

What sunk in early on was how quickly one can go from "Hero to Zero". You can be the most well-respected and hard-working officer on the department, but it only takes one negative incident to ruin your career forever. I knew how hard I had worked to get to that point in my life. All those years of college, the military, the academy, working several part-time jobs while going to school. There was no way I was going to let someone ruin it all for me. I knew that I had to stay away from bad situations, bad places, and bad people if I wanted to survive a long law enforcement career. Because let's face it. When you're a cop, a target is on your back on and off-duty. Don't make it any easier for them.

One of the coolest things about being a police officer was how easy it was to make people laugh. I mean, nobody has better stories than a cop. When you deal with the worst people on their worst day on a non-stop basis, the "cop-stories" are endless. And when you're dealing with human beings under stress, those stories often end in a comical way. It's just the nature of police work. I recall being at a Christmas party one evening. There were a bunch of people there who likely had many initials behind their name and quite honestly, looked much smarter than me. It was a crowd of medical people, and some were doctors. They were "talking shop", and the laughter was light, and at times, uncomfortable. Suddenly, one of them picked up on the fact that I was not part of the medical profession. It must have been pretty obvious, as I didn't know any of these people. They asked what I did for a living, and I told them I was a police officer. They gave you that look that many people give you when you tell them that. The questions ended up turning into a series of cop stories. Cop stories, as you can imagine can sometimes be graphic and utterly ridiculous. The girl I was with started kicking me under the table, urging me to stop. But it was clear to me that they were enjoying the free entertainment, so I continued on. I went from an outsider to the life of the party. Simply because of my occupation.

What I figured out quickly was how much interest there was in police work. The media is absolutely obsessed with it. At least half of their articles are in some way related to law enforcement. People love stories about crime. I think it's because it's as close to real life as it gets. It affects people from all walks of life. And to be blunt, it's very exciting. That's one of the things that attracted me to police work, originally. The fact that every day is different. Although you deal with a lot of the same calls, they're all unique in their own way.

When new officers would come on, I'd try to have a sit-down session with them, and warn them of the things that could potentially ruin their careers. I told them to watch who they hung out with. Watch who they get into relationships with. Watch their off-duty conduct in general. If you marry, live with, or have children with a girlfriend / boyfriend, under

Ohio Revised Code, you now have what's known as a "family or household member" relationship with that person. What that means legally is if you get into a violent situation with that person, it's now considered Domestic Violence under Ohio law. If you're actually convicted of Domestic Violence, you cannot possess a firearm under federal or state law. That means your law enforcement career is now over. Another example is getting arrested for OVI. If you're arrested for OVI, you likely will lose your license, which you obviously need to drive a police cruiser. So you can see how off-duty decisions can drastically affect your career.

I think one of the most important things to remember when it comes to your off-duty life is to make sure that you have one. Far too many cops work ridiculous hours, leaving them no time away from the daily madness. I would see many of them force themselves into having to do that. You can't live the life of a lawyer on a cop's salary. You just can't. If you try to, it'll take its toll on you one way or another.

Officers should have civilian friends. They should have hobbies and interests outside of police work. Those things remind you of what "normal life" is like. It is absolutely essential to keep in touch with old friends. Surviving a career in law enforcement depends on you surviving it both physically and emotionally. No matter how healthy you are physically, you can't enjoy retirement if your mind is shot.

If you are married to a police officer, or if you're simply a friend or family member of a police officer, keep in mind that their life experience isn't "normal" by any means. Nobody should see the things that they see on a daily basis, year after year. Encourage them to take time off. Encourage them to have friends away from the department. Encourage them to stay physically and mentally healthy. Keep them alive by giving them a different perspective. It's certainly a very effective way that you can "Protect & Serve" without actually joining the police ranks yourself.

Chief Keith Moser purchased a book for all of his officers and encouraged them to read it. It was a great book called, "Emotional Survival For Law Enforcement" written by Dr. Kevin M. Gilmartin. It is a great read not only for officers but their friends and families. I only wished I would have read that book as a rookie instead of as a twenty-year veteran. It's a book about how to prepare yourself for the challenges you'll likely face during your police career that you never thought of before. As someone who is getting into the police ranks, you naturally think that your worst enemies are guns, knives, and bad guys. While that certainly is true, the hidden enemy can at times be yourself. The things you see can be horrific to say the least. They can change you forever and make you difficult to live with. Again, I wish I would have read this book as a rookie.

Photo: "Emotional Survival for Law Enforcement" by Dr. Kevin M. Gilmartin

Chapter Six
"Leadership"

At about fifteen years into my career, I decided to take the promotional exam for sergeant. My logic was simple. As a senior patrolman, I am constantly being asked questions by rookie officers, so I may as well get paid for it.

I took the exam along with fourteen other officers. There were six books to study prior to the exam. I read one chapter of one book. My philosophy was simple; After fifteen years on the streets, I should be able to pass without studying. Well, I underestimated how difficult it was. It definitely was no walk in the park. I somehow passed, scoring second place out of the group. I was told I would be promoted in a few months. I was excited, but nervous. Being a police officer is one thing. Being in charge of them is a huge step in responsibility.

In law enforcement, leadership is everything. Cops have egos. It's no secret. Unguided egos can lead to disaster for an agency and a community. That's where leadership comes into play. Leadership does not require rank, either. A senior patrolman can absolutely be a leader without wearing stripes. On the other hand, being promoted does not make one a leader, either.

Photo: Being "sworn-in" as a Sergeant by Mayor Frank Cicchinelli (Jan 2011)

Depending on the agency, promotional exams can vary. Some only require a written exam. Some test by way of both written exams and assessments. Some agencies magically promote an officer to the highest rank by waving some type of magic wand (politics).

When you swear in as a police supervisor, suddenly you're responsible for more than yourself. You suddenly have the added responsibility of managing officers on your shift. In a way, it's like going from single and no kids to married with children. Life has changed. You're a sergeant. People are going to come to you with questions. You're going to have to make decisions on the streets. And some of those decisions can affect people's lives forever.

One thing I realized really quick after being promoted was how much I did not know. Questions would come your way in regards to things you never dealt with before as a patrolman. As a supervisor, it's okay to not know the answer to a question from someone you're supposed to be helping. But it's not okay to tell someone that you don't know and leave it at that. It's your job to know. And if you don't know, you better find out. That's why your agency promoted you. That's why your position exists. To help others who need guidance.

Lt Jason Greenfield was my immediate supervisor for many years while I was a sergeant. He taught me a lot about leadership and about life in general. One thing he told me really stuck in my mind. He told me that as a supervisor, you should be ready to do absolutely anything for your officers, including shining their shoes. Initially, I thought that was very strange, but I quickly figured out what his message was. He was telling them that he would do anything for them, but he simply expected a lot out of them in return. He never spoke down to people on the streets and he never did that with those under his command, either.

Photo: Lt Greenfield placing a rose for fallen Stark County law enforcement officers.

He certainly had a way with people. Once in a great while, our egos would clash and we would get upset at one another. One of us would always break the silence and put it behind us. We both were unable to stay mad at someone. I would always tell him that I wasn't sure if that was a strength or a weakness. He said it was a strength. I tend to agree. I was blessed to be able to work for someone like that. I really was.

As a rookie officer, I recall watching senior patrolman in the field. It was so obvious that they knew their stuff. You could see it in the way they carried themselves on calls. Their confidence was extremely obvious, and criminal suspects notice things like that. Trust me. As a rookie officer, it also made me more confident knowing they were at my side on the streets. That was one of the things I will always remember about my time at MPD; That you were never alone out there. Never. Ever. Were you left alone.

Photo: I was on a traffic stop one day, and asked for back-up. Within thirty seconds, this was what I saw. When you called, the Cavalry came and they came quickly.

It is a well-known fact that the best way to lead is by example. I was always of the belief that you should rarely ever have to tell an officer to do something. Want him or her to make more OVI arrests? It's simple. Make some yourself. Want your officers to do more community outreach activities? Go work some of them yourself. They say that imitation is the sincerest form of flattery. That's so true. If someone imitates you, they subconsciously want to be like you. So as a supervisor, you can see how your words and actions can easily influence others in either a positive or negative way. Which path you use is in your hands.

I was lucky enough to cross paths with people who left an impression on me during my career, and one of those people was Sheriff George Maier. Sheriff Maier was my safety director for a short period of time, but during his time there, I got to know him enough to know that he was very dedicated to law enforcement. He came from a family of law enforcement officers. I recall one day that I was speaking to my fellow officers and referred to them as "my guys". He took me to the side shortly thereafter and told me to always refer to them as "my officers". He explained that as a female officer, you may feel excluded. I remember being impressed not only by the advice given, but the fact that he took the time to correct me away from my peers. It also told me that he truly cared about people and how they feel. Those are traits of an effective leader. I was sad to see him leave to be the Sheriff of Stark County, but was glad to see that he was the chief law enforcement officer in the county that me, my family and many of my friends reside in.

Photo: SCSO Major Tim George, MPD Officer Fred Alexander, myself, Sheriff George T Maier, and Officer Dennis Muntean (SRO for Canal Fulton PD).

One of the hardest things about being a supervisor is that you cannot complain downward. You can only complain to those above you in rank. Often I'd catch myself saying things to officers that I should not have said. It's a long learning process. That's for sure. It's like anything else; You learn by screwing it up the first time. The key thing is: It's okay to make mistakes. Just acknowledge them when you do. You'll gain respect from those you're supposed to be guiding along the way. Most police officers are pretty sharp. They pay attention to mannerisms by the nature of the work they do. You're not going to fool them. Remember that they get lied to for a living just like you do.

One of my pet peeves from upper command staff in police departments across the country is when a chief or captain gives a statement to the media in regards to a complaint against an officer, or a video posted online alleging misconduct of somesort, and they are quick to make judgements against the officer before the investigation is even completed. When a police executive does that, they're doing no justice to the officer or the community. A police chief is charged with many responsibilities, but one important function is to be a liason to civilians who simply do not understand use of force situations. They need to educate the public when necessary. In the age of non-stop video footage and online "cop-bashing", civilians suddenly become law enforcement experts even though they've never worn a police uniform other than for Halloween.

If your officer is right, then say he or she is right. Explain why. Remember that you're talking to people who have likely never served in law enforcement. To bow to pressure and potentially harm an officer's career without having all of the facts is simply wrong. And it does no good for the public or the law enforcement profession as a whole. Same goes for mayors and other politicians when they're asked to comment on law enforcement issues. There is nothing wrong with saying that you are ignorant when it comes to law enforcement use of force, and other law enforcement topics as a civilian. Being ignorant is acceptable. It simply means you do not know something. Again, some of the most intelligent people know what they don't know and will admit it. I'd love to see more politicians and members of the media follow that basic concept. Onward.

Leadership in police work can be sticky at times. You can be asked to make some tough decisions in the field. Some of them may not be very popular, but often the right thing to do isn't the easy thing to do. I always used this rule of thumb even as a young officer assigned to midnight shift. When faced with a decision on the streets, and you're not so sure about what department policy or the Ohio Revised Code said, ask yourself this; If something was brought to the attention of the media in regards to the situation at hand, would your actions or inactions be judged as "reasonable" by the public? And don't be afraid to ask yourself, "What would God think?" I didn't have a perfect career by any means, but using that standard allowed me to retire after twenty-five years and walk away with a clear conscience.

One thing about leadership that I'd like to share; I'd often ask certain officers when they're taking the sergeant's exam. Many of them would reply, "No way. I'm not going to afternoons with Monday and Tuesday off". Or they'd give some other reason why they did not wish to be promoted. I'd usually reply by telling them, "Hey. This just in. It's not all about you". I wasn't insulting them. I was actually complimenting them. I was simply saying that they should put the organization and the profession in front of their own personal wants and wishes. In other words, I was telling them that I thought they'd make a great first-line supervisor, and that they should take a shot at it. You know who you are. I hope you're reading this.

Like many retired law enforcement officers, I still care. I care about the department that I worked for so many years. I care for the profession as a whole. I am confident that those in leadership positions will care, as well. As a law enforcement officer and as a police supervisor, it's your DUTY to care.

Photo: MPD "Eight-Point" hat traditionally worn by American police officers.

Chapter Seven
"Stories from the Streets"

"Cop Stories". Man, there are so many. Most cops could easily write a book about their experiences. The nature of police work makes it so easy. One thing I picked up on during the later years of my law enforcement career was that both the media and the general public seemed to be fascinated with police work. I can relate, because as a civilian in my mid-teens, I was obsessed with it, as well. I had no idea what a pension was. But the thought of working in a marked police car for the majority of my adult life was very exciting. I suppose that's because as a police officer, you're dealing with real things. Real-life situations. Life and death is a part of your daily routine. You see the element of human emotion (and stupidity) on a daily basis. The truth of it is that you see things that people simply should not see.

Some of the funniest things I ever witnessed in my life were during my law enforcement career. That comes as no surprise though, as police work involves human interaction. You then add the fact that those human beings are likely under stress during their police encounter, and the rest falls into place. On top of that, you add the emotions of fear, excitement, and anger. Alcohol, drugs and non-stop lies certainly can spice things up, as well.

I'll start off with my first foot pursuit. I had mentioned this story earlier, but with minimal details. Let me preface this with the fact that as a rookie, I did not have a very good concept of my geography. I grew up in Canton South, and spent a good amount of my childhood in Canton. Even if you grew up in a certain city, you likely only ever saw a very small portion of the actual neighborhood streets that you'd one day patrol.

I was in field training, and was speaking to a young male who I was trying to identify. I suspected he had a warrant or two, and was waiting for the information to come back from the dispatcher via LEADS. I noticed him looking around as I was waiting on the dispatcher. They tell you in the academy to watch their eyes, because that will tell you if they're going to run or fight. Well, the signs were there for me to see, but I wasn't paying attention. Next thing I know, he was running like a deer. He had at least a ten step lead on me. Now don't forget that I was wearing about twenty-plus extra pounds of gear, so he had a huge advantage on me in addition to the fact that he was fast and I wasn't. It was like a Smart Car trying to catch a Mustang G.T. 5.0. No chance.

That was, until he tripped and fell. I was able to jump on top of him and at this point, dispatch is calling me and repeatedly asking me for my location. I wasn't answering, so they assumed I was in trouble. The reason I wasn't answering was because I had absolutely no clue where I was. I thought quickly, figuring that the suspect was likely at his address where he fell. I screamed into his ear, "What's your address???!!" After deafening him the second time, he gave in and told me. I advised dispatch of my location, by simply giving his address, and hoped he wasn't lying. Sure enough, backup showed up, so I guess my trick worked. A few officers asked why I wasn't answering my radio. I simply replied, "Man, I was out of breath. I couldn't even talk". After getting the suspect into the cruiser, I leaned against the car, exhausted. I then threw up in front of my fellow officers. Yeah, I'm sure they were really impressed. I never did tell them the truth as to how I figured out where I was. I guess that's part of being a good cop. Thinking on your feet.

In police work, you have to be able to laugh at yourself. Trust me. I did it daily. Although there is a lot of negativity that you're exposed to, there is also a lot to laugh and smile about. Take Canal Fulton P.D. Chief Doug Swartz as an example. Doug loved being a cop. Like myself, he chased a career in law enforcement since his early teens. That was what he wanted to, and nothing was going to stop him from wearing that badge one day. Doug loved being a cop. He was very aggressive, going after drunks, drugs, and guns. When you're aggressive, you end up in pursuits. It's not if they'll run, it's when. And how long. How fast, and how dangerous will that pursuit be? Those are the only questions.

Photo: CFPD Chief Doug Swartz (Credit Massillon Independent)

Doug was a patrolman at the time, and had initiated one of his many traffic stops. The driver fled, and speeds quickly exceeded one hundred miles per hour. The suspect lost control of his vehicle like they often do, and went into a ditch. The vehicle went airborne, and landed upside down. Doug approached the driver's side of the vehicle, thinking the driver was pinned inside. He's screaming at the driver,

"Sir, are you okay??!" He got no answer. He asked repeatedly, trying to get a response from the suspect, thinking the worst had happened. Eventually he hears a voice saying, "Yes...are you okay?". Doug says, "Yes, I'm fine....are you okay, sir??". This exchange went back and forth several times until he hears, "Uh, yes....I'm fine. This is OnStar". At this point, Doug realizes that the crash activated the OnStar system, and the suspect had already fled on foot. Again, you have to be able to laugh at yourself. It happens to the best of us.

Case in point: I never lived this next ridiculous story down: In my defense, I was sent to this call. I did not look for it. I was dispatched to the area of the Speedway (Super America) to check for possible DUI / OVI involving a horse and buggy. I located the "suspect" behind the gas station and called it out over the radio. I recall an unnamed Sergeant making horse sounds on the radio. I knew at this point that this was about to go really bad. I hit the overhead lights and the horse and buggy stopped in a dark alley. I quickly figured out that the Amish boy in his teens was under the influence of alcohol and was in control of the "vehicle", which made it an OVI / DUI by legal definition. After a series of Standard Field Sobriety Tests, I placed the kid under arrest and placed him into my police cruiser.

A curious (nosey) citizen overhead another officer and myself discussing what we were going to do with the horse and buggy. I knew that I could not tow it, so I was desperate for a solution. The neighbor said that he would volunteer to secure the horse and buggy while the kid was getting booked at the city jail. Having no other options, I took him up on his offer. That was my second mistake.

As I am later booking the juvenile, a sergeant leans over my shoulder and asks where I made the arrest on the horse and buggy. I said, "Behind Super America...why, ma'am?" She said, "Oh okay, well that explains why we just got a call that a horse and buggy is loose and running around the gas pumps, scaring all the customers". My heart started pounding. I was sweating bullets trying to figure out what my letter to the chief would say explaining this mess I got myself into. And yes, that made the news.

Photo: Massillon Independent article describing another one of my famous arrests.

As you all know, criminals aren't the smartest species on the planet. I was sent to a shoplifter call at one of the local retail stores. Prior to arriving on scene, radio advised that the shoplifter was running from store security. As I pulled up, I saw him running northbound. I stopped the cruiser in traffic and started chasing him on foot. I wasn't gaining on him, but I saw that he was running towards a local juvenile detention facility. I thought to myself, "There is no way he's gonna going to run into that place. Sure enough, he did. He ran from the police, and ran right into a state prison for juvenile offenders. The guard on duty opened the door for a shoplifter, but I had to convince him to open it up for me (in full uniform). I thought to myself, "Did that seriously just happen??"

Resisting arrest. Such a terrible choice one makes. When you take a look at police contacts with citizens, the overwhelming majority of them end without incident. When people comply with police orders, things usually go pretty smoothly. On the other hand, when one makes that selfish decision to challenge the validity of an arrest on the streets, things go south and they do so very quickly. Now don't get me wrong, cops make mistakes. At times, they make bad arrests. They're human beings. You won't find any profession with a perfect batting average. It simply does not exist in the real world. In addition, police work is not a perfect science. There are so many variables that simply cannot be controlled. But for some reason, the media and the Monday Morning Quarterbacks cannot comprehend that. Or, perhaps they simply do not want to. I do know this though; Resisting arrest is a choice. And it's a bad choice. It's a decision that can very easily lead to your death. Allow me to give you an example; a police officer has you stopped on the side of a highway. He says those three words that nobody wants to hear: You're under arrest. You decide to resist your arrest. The next thing you know, you're struggling on the side of a highway. The officer loses his / her balance, and falls in front of a car weighing five thousand pounds traveling at one hundred feet per second. The officer is crushed, and dies as a result of the decision that you made. Guess what? You're not going to jail. You're going to prison. And you're now a convicted felon. Or perhaps you fell into the path of a semi during the struggle and your life is suddenly over. That one bad decision has now changed your life forever, or simply ended your life.

People often ask why people keep stealing. Well, I'll tell you why. Because there are no ramifications for theft. When I started in police work, the Ohio Revised Code stated that if you were previously convicted of a theft offense, the second time you were caught stealing (regardless of the value of the products or services), it was a fourth degree felony. That meant you faced the possibility of prison time if you were caught twice in your adult life. Well, I come to work one day, and suddenly the law had changed. The enhancement section was removed. So now under ORC 2913.02 (Theft), as long as the value of the property is less than $1,000, you can go into any department store, steal $999.99 worth of merchandise, and do it twenty times a day for the rest of your life. It will never become a felony. And trust me that the thieves know this. That's one reason why they keep stealing. This is just one law of many that makes absolutely no sense at all to me as a retired police officer or as a citizen. I'd arrest females and their purse was stuffed with stolen merchandise. Nothing in that purse whatsoever except stolen goods. That told me that they came into the store with an empty purse. Now tell me what woman carries an empty purse? We all know the answer to that question: None. That tells me that they came into the store with the sole purpose to steal. An empty purse is called "Criminal Tools" under Ohio law, because it's a device specifically used to commit a criminal offense. Sorry about your luck, lady. What color of bracelets would you like on your wrists? Silver or black?

When I was in the academy, the instructors would always tell us to watch a person's reaction when they notice your presence. That will tell you a lot about who they are and what they were up to just before you arrived. One thing I always paid attention to was how people would suddenly start smoking when they saw a uniformed officer. And some would almost inhale the entire cigarette in thirty seconds. You knew they were extremely nervous and something was not right. I'd usually walk up to them and ask them, "What's your warrant for?". Often they'd come right out and tell me because it was beyond obvious.

Domestics. We've all heard about how dangerous domestic violence calls can be for responding officers. Statistically, they can be one of the most dangerous calls in police work. I have my theories why that is. You're usually mixing alcohol with emotions, access to weapons (guns and kitchen knives), and the fact that often people feel empowered in their own homes. In addition, even though you're called there to fix their problems, often they don't like to see someone they love go out the door in handcuffs, and suddenly you're the target of the violence. Domestic Violence is ugly. It's wrong. It has long-lasting effects on the kids who often are right in the middle of adults acting like children, unfortunately. Those types of calls are certainly something that I do not miss whatsoever.

I would often tell officers not to stay on midnights too long. They're bad for your health. They're unhealthy for your relationships, and it's probably the most dangerous shift / assignment at most departments. Police work by nature is dangerous and we all understand that when we swear in, but you really want to manage it during your career. I did about half of my career on midnights, and although it was a true life experience, it certainly took its toll on my life in many ways. Give and take, I suppose.

On the other hand, there certainly is a lot to laugh at on midnights. You're dealing with the worst human beings on their worst day, and often they're high and/or drunk. I recall one evening, I arrested a female for OVI. She kept howling like a wolf. She was howling during the booking process and continued to howl all the way to the jail. I recall looking up to the sky at 2am, and seeing a bright full moon. At that time,

"Bark at the Moon" by Ozzy Osbourne comes on the radio. I just kept my eyes on the road as I drove down US62, and thought to myself, "My Mom told me to be a math teacher. I should have listened to her."

Although midnight shift was very hard on your mind and body, and likely took years off my life, I learned so much. I learned about how evil the world can be at times. At the same time, it gave me the chance to stand up for those who were wronged in some way. It gave me the chance to go after OVI offenders who hurt other people and ruined lives. I am truly blessed to have been able to experience that in my life. I saw those years as another gift from God.

At the same time, there are some memories that stick out. Let me share a funny one with you before I go onto the next chapter. Officer Miguel Riccio would always be there when I made an OVI arrest. He was obviously there for my safety, but there's another part to the story.

Photo: Officer Miguel Riccio and K-9 "Inca"

Miguel was obsessed with Dunkin Donut coffee. At the time, Massillon did not have a Dunkin' Donuts. The closest one was in Canton on the way to the Stark County Jail. Miguel knew that if I made an arrest, I would soon be passing his favorite place on the way back. So as Miguel pulled up to my traffic stop, he would discreetly get his wallet out while he was looking around to see who was watching. I started feeling guilty like I did something wrong. Next thing I know he secretly passes me a couple bucks while looking around, and whispers, "Ay Munsta...get me a medium with cream and shooga" with his strong Spanish accent. He would do this every time like clockwork. It was comical. It's one of those great memories I have of MIguel. I love that guy. All the MPD officers loved when he would tell stories. Nobody told a story like Miguel. I miss MIguel. I hope he retires and enjoys life. He deserves it. Everyone said to me when I retired, "You won't miss the streets, but you'll miss the guys." Very true. Very true, indeed.

Chapter Eight
"Signal Two"

You're probably trying to figure out why I named this final chapter "Signal Two". Allow me to explain. "Signal Two" at MPD was radio code for "complete". In other words, you have cleared the call, and you're now ready for the next assignment. I think it was an appropriate title for this chapter. In more ways than one.

As I approached the day when I was eligible to retire, I obsessed over it. Should I? Shouldn't I? It seemed like a simple decision. After all, I never read a gravestone that read, "I WISH I WORKED LONGER". At the same time, I'd be leaving a job that I truly loved. One thing I thought about was this: You only have one life, and there's a lot out there to do besides police work. And I'm not going to lie. Those 04:30 wake-ups were not my thing. The birds are supposed to wake us up. Not the opposite.

So one thing I wanted to stress in this chapter is how much I appreciated my fellow officers during my career. Had it not been for them being there every time I needed them, I would have never made it. I told them at both of my retirement parties that I owed them everything. I will never forget how they were there. Every single time. Not once in my long career was I left alone in a dangerous position. That means the world to me. I can't stress that any more.

Photo: They sent me off with a very nice party, a generous Best Buy gift card, and a bag of my favorite chips.

I am very certain that they will continue to be there for one another during their careers. That is the beauty of police work. Although there are not enough of them out there, they travel in packs. Like wolves. They do that by design. So when you're stopped by a police officer, and maybe one or two more marked cars drive by and give you that look like they're checking you out, just know that they're checking on their fellow officer who wants to go home and tuck his / her kids into bed at night. It's nothing personal. It's about survival.

Often people ask, "If you had to do it all over again, knowing what you know now, would you do it again?" The answer is that I absolutely would. They usually follow up with a question like, "Would you do anything differently?" I would say that's irrelevant. It happened the way it was supposed to happen. That was God's plan.

Photo: My MPD-issued Smith & Wesson M&P 9mm duty weapon, which was issued to me for the cost of $1 at retirement. Engraved with my name, rank, badge number, and years of service.

On the other hand, I would offer advice to those going in. If you're going to join the police ranks, do it for the right reasons. Don't do it because you need a job. Or you want a government job. You likely will not survive your career, and it could end very badly for you. Do it because you honestly want to make a difference. Not that you want to change the world, because you can't. But because you want to change someone else's world. Now you can absolutely do that.

As a police officer, you absolutely have that ability. The worst thing you can do as a cop is to show up for work and do the minimum. You may think you're getting away with something, but you're really not. You're slowly dying is what you're doing. Now don't get me wrong. Very few officers are as aggressive in their twentieth year that they are in their third year, including myself. That's just nature. But do more than what you're expected to do. That's the key to a successful career. And you'll sleep better at night knowing that you did something for society with that day that was given to you.

Photo: Officer Teddy Hyatt inhaling some BW3's wings. Teddy is a SRO for Massillon City Schools. Teddy is always laughing. He laughs so much, it would make me laugh, which made him laugh even harder. It was a vicious cycle. Be safe, Teddy...

One thing that really made me smile the other day: I saw several of our new officers taking on the extra role of getting involved with the community. Playing basketball with the kids. Getting out of the car and speaking to those whom they serve. Officer Teddy Hyatt promised to be active on the MPD Facebook site. I saw Officer Jerrell Vincent in the newspaper, talking about police work.

Photo: Officer Jerrell Vincent. Jerrell came on as I was retiring. I told him he'll have a great career. He has a natural ability to communicate with people.

Someone joked and called him "Muntean Junior". That made me laugh, but it also made me smile. It made me think that perhaps I did rub off on them a little bit. That the great relationship that we worked so hard to obtain over the years will continue. I saw that Sgt Jes Harting got the National Night Out going again. Those are all great things. It truly made me smile. It really did.

I remember speaking to Officer Jamie Slutz and Chief Keith Moser one day about the unique relationship that Massillon P.D. has with those whom the department serves. We were all in agreement that Massillon has a great thing going, but it takes work and dedication to make sure that it lasts. I believe they will continue to do just that. In my opinion (and mine may be biased), I believe that MPD leads the way in Stark County when it comes to community relations.

Photo: During my career, people would always mistake me for Officer Jamie Slutz. My Aunt saw him once and swore it was me. It happened daily. We both had fun with it. I bet he's using my name-plate after I retired. Jamie is now a Detective for MPD.

And this chapter would not be complete without some discussion about the citizens of Massillon, Ohio. I always said we didn't have forty-some officers. We had forty-some officers and tens of thousands of law-abiding citizens who were very willing to help when called upon. And that is the absolute truth. If we posted a photo of a wanted suspect, they were on it. We would get tips via phone calls, emails, Facebook messages, you name it. We solved a lot of cases with the help of the public, and some were major cases.

Photo: One of the many tokens of thanks from our wonderful citizens. They were there for us when many were against us.

On top of that, for nearly my last five years years on the job, they brought us goodies, paid for our meals while we ate out, paid for our drinks in the drive-thru line, or would simply approach us in public and thank us for our service. That meant so much to us when others were attacking us from every angle. Believe me when I say that we noticed.

The kids from "ChopStix" restaurant drew a picture of me. They once said to me, "You're really skinny and your head looks like a potato". I was speechless and kept looking in the mirror for the next couple days.

One thing I would always tell new officers is the following: The only reason that forty-some police officers can police thirty-three thousand people is because they let you. And the only reason they let you is because they respect you and they trust you. Do not ever lose that trust and respect either as an individual officer or as a department. Once you do, your job will become much more difficult and the world will be a tough place to live.

In closing, I would just like to thank my fellow officers and the citizens for treating me so well during my time as a police officer in Tiger Town, USA.

God Bless. Peace…

Sgt B Muntean (Retired)

Twenty-five years of peaks and valleys...

Photo: As a tradition, MPD officers walk through the rank and file on their last day on duty. This is me walking out the door on my last day. Great memories…

Beth Bennethum, her son, Corey (Volunteer for MPD) and retired MFD Firefighter Mike Stone at our annual Bikin' with Badges community bike ride. Good times…

Darren Hodgson. I met Darren while on patrol one day. He bought my lunch and gave me this "Thin Blue Line" pocket knife.. A Veteran and a gentleman. Darren passed away a few months before I retired. God Bless Darren and his family.

This is Austin. I met him during my last year as a police officer. He's a wonderful kid. He loves police officers. He named his lion after me. Great kid from a great family.

I took this aerial picture of Paul Brown Tiger Stadium a few months after I retired. Once you retire, you find other passions. I love photography, and I must admit that drones are very addicting. Go Tigers!

Travel after you retire. The world is a big place. This is a walking path I checked out while vacationing near Ramstein Air Base in Germany. Absolutely beautiful country, indeed.

This is Dennis "Porkchop" Smith on his birthday. Dennis is one of MPD's SROs (School Resource Officer). We were on some tough calls together. Dennis is a great guy. Be safe, Porkchop…

MPD Officer Ryan Wood. Ryan was hired on a few years before I retired. He's a gentleman. He's polite, and humble. He does his job well. Police departments need more people like Ryan. Be safe, Woody…

Cliff Franks made me a retirement mug out of this picture. Cliff was one of those people I was blessed to cross paths with. Very talented. And he has five kids while he does everything else. What a multi-tasker!

My nephew and Godson (Jackson). He's my little buddy.

Det Shaun Dadisman is surrounded by his fellow officers when he was awarded "Officer of the Year".

I want to say this is a 2013 Ford Police Interceptor. I really loved the design of our new police cruisers. We actually won a cruiser design contest / car show sponsored by Jackson PD that year.

What a crew…

Officer Jeff Crawford...we were hired together. Jeff was our traffic officer for many years. Jeff will be retiring very soon. Be safe, Craw-Daddy!!

Officer Kervin Brown and I were hired together. Kervin recently retired a few months after me. Glad he made it...

The MPD Ballers…

Officer Gary McPherson..he and Officer Tom Minarcheck were the first MPD Bike Patrol officers. Gary left MPD and went into education.

Sgt Wes Esper retired not long after I was hired. He always worked O.T. for me so I could ride my motorcycle on sunny days…

Officer Miguel Riccio and Officer Dennis "Porkchop" Smith manning the jail on midnight shift…

Inca's birthday….he ordered his steak medium rare.

Inside of my patrol car (M-103) right before I retired. They started looking like something from Star Wars. I knew it was time to go…

Two new F-150s were getting prepped for the street…

Officer Derick Spangler and Sgt Tom Rogers took the time to say hello to a little girl watching the Memorial Day parade…

Lookin' sharp on Memorial Day...

Officer Caleb Ogletree, Officer Samantha Stuhm, and Officer Kervin Brown at Police Week festivities in Washington, DC…

Memorial Day Parade in downtown Massillon. Lookin' sharp like usual…

"Batman & Robin" AKA Officer Sherman Kruger and Officer Mike Manos…

Lt Jason Greenfield, Lt Mike Maier, Sgt Jes Harting, Sgt Josh Edwards, myself, and Chief Keith Moser at the annual fallen officers memorial in Canton, Ohio.

Honorable Judge Ed Elum: A true American. He served in the U.S. Navy, and is responsible for building the beautiful Veteran's Memorial Park next to the city hall complex. I would see him out there every Saturday morning watering all of the trees and shrubs, and he always made it a priority to maintain it to honor those who sacrificed everything for our great nation. Thank you for your service, Judge.

The biggest bust of my career: The day I arrested Spiderman.

My best friend (Dean Mugnaini). We met in the 5th grade when he wrecked my sandcastle. We went to Canton South together. We were always up to no good. Dean is now a father to three beautiful kids and is happily married to his wife, Rebecca. Dean served in the US Army as an 11Bravo (Infantry). He went on to have a successful career with the US Postal Service.. Again, we were far from perfect as kids, but we both ended up doing okay in life. Proof that nobody is looking for angels.

"Three Wildcats". Myself, Lt Dennis Garren (Canton PD), and my brother Officer Dennis Muntean (CFPD). All Canton South Alumni…

My dad adopted me when I was three. I always told him he saved my life, as fathers are so important to a child's upbringing. He was shoveling our driveway on the SW side of Canton during the Blizzard of '78 in this picture. Love you, Dad...

God Bless those who gave "The Ultimate Sacrifice" protecting others. I truly believe there is a special place in Heaven for each one of them. God Bless...